The Passion of
St Edmund

Published by the Langley Press, 2018

© 2018 Simon Webb. The right of Simon Webb to be
identified as the Author of the Work has been asserted by him in
accordance with the Copyright, Designs and Patents Act 1988.
All rights reserved.

The cover shows The Martyrdom of St Edmund,
from British Library Manuscript Royal 2 B VI,
England, thirteenth century

The Passion of
St Edmund

by

Abbo of Fleury

Translated by

Francis Hervey

Also from the Langley Press

The Legend of the Three Kings

The Legend of St Cuthbert

In Search of the Celtic Saints

In Search of the Northern Saints

A Little Book of English Saints

For free downloads and more from the
Langley Press, please visit our website at
http://tinyurl.com/lpdirect

Contents

St Dunstan, from British Library Manuscript
Royal 10 A XIII, England, twelfth century

Introduction

From time to time St Dunstan, a celebrated tenth-century Archbishop of Canterbury, liked to re-tell a tale he had heard from a very old man, whose name has now been lost to history, like a name scratched into the wet sand of a beach.

The old man had claimed to have been the armour-bearer of Edmund, king of East Anglia. His story was an eye-witness account of the death of Edmund at the hands of what we would now call the Vikings. The manner of Edmund's death, and the miracles that followed it, as reported by the elderly veteran, suggested that King Edmund deserved to be included, with St Margaret of Scotland and St Oswald of Northumbria, in the list of royal British saints.

One man who heard the white-haired Archbishop Dunstan re-tell the story of the Passion and posthumous miracles of St Edmund was Abbo of Fleury, a distinguished French monk and scholar who spent a couple of years in England from 985 to 987 CE. Abbo was charged with setting up a school in the monastery of Ramsey in Cambridgeshire: while he was there, he re-told his friend Dunstan's story about Edmund, and the Ramsey monks begged him to write it down. Since his was probably the first attempt to put the tale on paper, Abbo's Latin prose Passion of St Edmund marks the moment at which a piece of oral tradition became a written text.

In the nearly one hundred and twenty years between the death of King Edmund and the day Abbo picked up his pen, Edmund's story had acquired miraculous elements that it will be difficult for some modern, scientifically-minded readers to take at face value. Chief among these is the miracle whereby the severed head of Edmund is able to cry out to the good folks who are searching for it, and guide them to the right place. There, in the depths of a forest, the head is found to be being guarded by a gigantic wolf, whose nature has been made gentle by the presence of the saint. (In a book on Edmund published in 1970, Bryan Houghton suggested that what really happened on that day was that the king's head was being guarded by one of his wolf-*hounds*, which barked to attract the searchers.)

Other miracles recounted by Abbo include the freedom from decay of Edmund's body (its 'incorruption'), and the madness, joined later by physical illness, inflicted on one Leofstan, who insisted on looking at the body. Leofstan is also cursed with poverty because of his morbid curiosity, and his own body becomes infested with worms, like those of two of the Herods mentioned in the New Testament.

Eight robbers who attempt to steal the treasures around Edmund's tomb at night are also miraculously frozen in various interesting poses, so that they can be caught first thing in the morning. Bishop Theodred orders that they should all be hanged, but soon regrets his cruel sentence.

Abbo's account lacks some of the additional miraculous details recounted in later versions, for instance in John Lydgate's fifteenth-century English poem about St Edmund and St Fremund. Abbo could not have included these in his own account simply because they hadn't happened yet: miracles continued to surround Edmund's body long after both Abbo and Dunstan had passed away. Perhaps the most memorable of these later miracles has to do with an attempt by one Bishop Alphun of London to steal Edmund's body and place it in St Paul's Cathedral. To frustrate the bishop, the saint made his coffin as heavy as a great hill of stone; but when someone came to return the body to Bury St Edmund's, it became light and manoeuvrable again.

Abbo, the author of Edmund's Passion, shared more than an interest in St Edmund with his friend St Dunstan, to whom he dedicated his account of the royal martyr's death. Both were committed to reforming both the monasteries and the Church of their time, and both were profound scholars. Both also had a habit of writing such clever Latin that it sometimes puzzled their readers.

One outcome of Abbo's decision to couch his Passion of St Edmund in sophisticated language was that later authors misunderstood his assertion that, as seems likely, Edmund was descended from a Saxon family that had been present in England for several generations. Some read Abbo's words as meaning that Edmund had been *born in Saxony*: it then became necessary to think up a story that 'covered' the saint's birth in Germany and explained how he became king of East Anglia.

In Lydgate's version, Offa, an elderly, childless king of East Anglia, travels to Saxony and meets his nephew, Edmund. Finding the boy beyond all praise, he adopts him, and Edmund soon inherits his uncle's kingdom. Lydgate goes on to give us a great deal of detail about how well Edmund ruled East Anglia, and describes how his martial prowess enabled him to defeat the invading Danes in an important battle near Thetford. This wealth of detail about Edmund contrasts with the very small amount of reliable evidence we have about him from historical records such as the Anglo-Saxon Chronicle.

Because Abbo does not include such details as the

probably spurious personal reasons that the Vikings Ivar and Ubba had for invading England, which are included in later accounts, his own treatment of the story of Edmund comes up a little short. This may be why he does include information about why he is writing the story down, and where he heard it in the first place. He also gives us a brief history of the Anglo-Saxon race in England, makes time to compare Edmund to earlier saintly and biblical figures, and tries to allay any concerns his readers might have about the truth of some elements of his tale.

Near the end of his narrative, Abbo also attempts to explain how the soul of a saint like Edmund can be simultaneously in heaven and also in or near his body, working miracles.

It is possible that Abbo of Fleury, whose book on Edmund was a valuable source for later writers on the subject, was in England in the 980s because he had failed to be elected as abbot of Fleury. In 988 this mistake was put right, and the new abbot applied his large and versatile brain to the business of running an important abbey, while still finding time to write, often on scientific subjects.

We cannot know whether Abbo ever looked through the pages of a personal copy of his Passion of Edmund: if he did, he is unlikely to have regarded any part of it as a prophecy of his own end. But like the English King Edmund, the Frenchman did suffer a violent death. He died shortly after being fatally injured while trying to intervene in a quarrel between the monks of La Réole in Gascony and the local townspeople. This happened on the thirteenth of November 1004.

The following translation of Abbo's *Passio* is the one printed by Francis Hervey in his *Corolla Sancti Eadmundi* (Garland of St Edmund), published by John Murray in 1907.

Hervey's dignified English reflects Abbo's elaborate Latin. In this edition, I have broken the translation into paragraphs to make it easier to follow, and given sub-headings to Abbo's numbered sections.

Simon Webb, Durham, August 2018

Dedication

Here begins the dedicatory epistle accompanying the
Passion of Saint Edmund, King and Martyr.

For Dunstan, Lord Archbishop of the holy metropolitan
Church of Canterbury, ripe, sooth to say, in character as in
age, Abbo of Fleury, a monk in deacon's orders, though
unworthy, bespeaks the dews of the blessing of Christ the
Lord above and below.

After I had departed from you, venerable father, with
much cheerfulness of heart, and had returned with haste to
the monastery that you wot of, the brethren, with whom,
being detained by their fraternal kindness, I have hitherto
been staying as a guest, began to press me urgently to
comply with their saintly desire, that I would reduce to
writing the Passion of the miracle-worker, Edmund, king
and martyr. This, they declared, would be edifying to future
generations, and acceptable to you, as well as a serviceable
memento of my humble self among the English churches.

They had heard, indeed, that the story of this Passion,
which is unknown to most people, and has been committed
to writing by none, had been related by your Holiness, as
collected from ancient tradition, in my presence, to the Lord

Bishop of Rochester, and to the Abbot of the monastery which is called Malmesbury, and to other brethren then assembled in accordance with your practice, whom you cease not to nourish with the food of God's word, alike in the Latin and in the mother tongue.

To them you averred, while the tears ran from your eyes, that you had in your youth learned the history from a broken-down veteran, who in relating it, simply and in good faith, to the most glorious English king, Athelstan, declared on his oath that, on the very day on which the martyr laid down his life for Christ's sake, he had been armour-bearer to the saintly hero.

In view of the great reliance which you placed on the old man's assertions, and which led you to store up his words in their entirety in the re-ceptacle of your memory, to be uttered at a later date with honeyed accents to a younger generation, the brethren insisted strongly, notwithstanding my diffidence, that I would satisfy their earnest desire, and to the best of my ability preserve from utter oblivion so important a series of events.

I felt that I could not with due self-respect refuse their request, and therefore, postponing for the moment the study of secular literature, I betook myself as it were to the esoteric wisdom of the spirit, and undertook to describe the good deeds of the king, who addicted himself on the throne of his kingdom to the truest philosophy, but especially those which, unparalleled in the world's history, were wrought after his death; to which none would give credence were they not vouched for by the irrefragable authority of your assertion.

In truth, when you, the snows of whose head compel belief, made mention of the still continuing incorruption of the king's body, one of those present anxiously raised the question whether such things were possible! In order to clear up the doubt involved in that question, you alleged, from the ample stores of your experience, the instance (which still more powerfully struck the astonished minds of your auditors) of Cuthbert, the Saint of the Lord, and incomparable Confessor and Bishop, who not only to this day awaits with body incorrupt the day of the first resurrection, but continues to be suffused with a gentle warmth.

In this I found an admirable proof, which led me with more assurance to the careful relation of the holy king's actions, inspired as I was with full trust in his and your incomparable merits. And so, in dedicating to you the first fruits of my labour, I humbly beseech you to be so good as to bestow upon me, if it be but one day of your leisure in so worthy a cause, retrenching what is in excess, and supplying what is in defect, since, with the exception of the last miracle of the series, I have in every particular composed the narrative, as you delivered it, faithfully following a faithful informant, and exhorting all to the love of so eminent a martyr.

Farewell, my Father in Christ.

Here ends the Epistle Dedicatory.

1. The Saxons, the Jutes, and the Angles

Summoned in times past to Britain to give, for a dubious reward, a fatal assistance, three tribes of Germany, namely, the Saxons, the Jutes, and the Angles, were at first and for a while protectors to the Britons.

Involved in frequent wars, they defended themselves and their clients with courage; but as the latter were given over to sloth, and stayed at home, as might be expected of a proletariat, absorbed in pleasure alone, trusting to the unconquered bravery of the hireling soldiery whom they had retained, the protectors took counsel for the expulsion from home and country of the wretched natives.

And so it was done; the Britons were turned out, and the alien conquerors set to work to parcel out among themselves the island, replete, as it was, with wealth of every kind, on the ground that it was a shame that it should be retained under the rule of a lazy populace, when it might afford a competent livelihood to men of mettle who were fit to defend themselves.

The occasion having thus arisen, the eastern part of the island, which, even to this day, is called 'Eastengle' in the speech of the Angles, fell to the lot of the Saxons, while the Jutes and Angles parted in other directions, in which they could follow the clues of their own fortunes, so that there should be no controversy with their comrades as to their possessions, the country being spacious enough to satisfy the needs of their several dominions.

Hence it came about that the single island of Britain was broken up into districts and provinces, and sufficed for a number, at first of leaders, and afterwards of kings.

II. East Anglia

But the above-mentioned eastern part attracts consideration for the following among other reasons, viz. that it is washed by waters on almost every side, girdled as it is on the south and east by the ocean, and on the north by an immense tract of marsh and fen, which starting, owing to the level character of the ground, from practically the midmost point of Britain, slopes for a distance of more than a hundred miles, intersected by rivers of great size, to the sea.

But on the side where the sun sets, the province is in contact with the rest of the island, and on that account accessible; but as a bar to constant invasion by an enemy, a foss sunk in the earth is fortified by a mound equivalent to a wall of considerable height.

In the interior the soil is rich and extremely productive, and delightfully pleasant with its gardens and woods, while it is noted for its excellent sport, and for its abundant grazing for flocks and herds. I pass over its rivers, which abound in fish, as on one side, as has been mentioned, the country is lapped by the sea, and on the other, where the marshes are spread out, stretch after stretch of the fen waters, as much as two or three miles in breadth, trickles past.

These marshes afford to not a few congregations of monks desirable havens of lonely life, in the seclusion of which solitude cannot fail the hermits, amongst whom may be mentioned the celibate and cenobite monks of the order of the holy father Benedict, in a spot that has now gained celebrity.

III. King Edmund

But, to revert to our subject, over this fertile province reigned the most holy, and, in God's sight, acceptable Prince Edmund. He was sprung from the noble stock of the Old Saxons, and from his earliest childhood cherished most sincerely the Christian faith. Descended from a line of kings, and endued with a high character, he was, by the unanimous choice of all his fellow-provincials, not so much elected in due course of succession, as forced to rule over them with the authority of the sceptre.

He was in truth of a comely aspect, apt for sovereignty; and his countenance continually developed fresh beauty through the tranquil devotion of his most serene spirit. To all he was affable and winning in speech, and distinguished by a captivating modesty; and he dwelt among his contemporaries with admirable kindness, though he was their lord, and without any touch of haughtiness or pride.

The holy Edmund did indeed already carry in his countenance what afterwards was made manifest by God's will; since even as a boy he grasped with whole-hearted endeavour the ladder of virtue, the summit of which he was destined by God's mercy to reach by martyrdom.

IV. A Golden Age

How beneficent he was in relation to his subjects, when he had been raised to the throne, and how strict in dealing with wrong-doers, it is beyond my abilities to describe; indeed I could not in suitable language set forth even the least of his merits. It may be said that he so combined the gentleness and simplicity of the dove with the wariness and sagacity of the serpent, that he was neither deceived by the fraudulent pretences of the old enemy of mankind, nor sanctioned the iniquitous sophisms of evilly-minded men.

Any matter of which he was ignorant he would investigate with the utmost industry; and proceeding along the royal road, he deviated neither to the right through too exalted a notion of his own merits, nor to the left by falling a victim to the faults of human frailty. In addition, he was liberal in his bounty to those in want, and like a benignant father to the orphan and the widow. He ever kept in view the dictum of the wise man: 'Have they made you a prince? be not exalted, but be among them as one of them.'

And so eminently conspicuous was he in the face of Christ and of the Church, through the adornment of good deeds, that, as in the case of Saint Job, to test his patience became the aim of the enemy of the human race, who cherishes a grudge against the good, which is all the deeper, because he lacks every impulse towards good-will.

V. The Coming of the Danes

With this object he despatched one of his own satellites as an adversary to Edmund, in the hope that, stripped of all his possessions, the king might be goaded into an outburst of impatience, and in despair curse God to His face.

This adversary was known by the name of Ivar; and he, with another called Ubba, a man of equal depravity, attempted (and nothing but the divine compassion could have prevented them) to reduce to destruction the whole confines of Britain. And no wonder! seeing that they came hardened with the stiff frost of their own wickedness from that roof of the world where he had fixed his abode who in his mad ambition sought to make himself equal to the Most High.

In fine it is proverbial, according to the prediction of the prophet, that from the north comes all that is evil, as those have had too good cause to know, who through the spite of fortune and the fall of the die have experienced the barbarity of the races of the north.

These, it is certain, are so cruel by the ferocity of their nature, as to be incapable of feeling for the ills of mankind; as is shown by the fact that some of their tribes use human flesh for food, and from the circumstance are known by the Greek name Anthropophagists.

Nations of this kind abound in great numbers in Scythia,

near the Hyperborean Mountains, and are destined, as we read, more than all other races, to follow Antichrist, and to batten without compunction on the agonies of men who refuse to bear on their foreheads the mark of the beast.

Hence it results that they can observe no truce in harrying the worshippers of Christ, and this is true especially of the Danes, who, dwelling fatally near to the western regions, indulge continually in piratical raids upon them. Of this nation were the generals Ivar and Ubba, whom I have mentioned above.

They set out in the first instance to attack the province of Northumbria, and overran the whole district from one end to the other, inflicting upon it the heaviest devastation. None of the inhabitants could resist these abominable onslaughts, but suffered the too well merited chastisement of the divine wrath through the instrumentality of Ubba the agent of iniquity.

Having raked together their booty, Ivar left on the spot Ubba. his associate in cruelty, and approaching suddenly with a great fleet, landed by stealth at a city in that region, entered it before the citizens were aware of his approach, and set it on fire.

Boys, and men old and young, whom he encountered in the streets of the city were killed, and he paid no respect to the chastity of wife or maid. Husband and wife lay dead or dying together on their thresholds; the babe snatched from its mother's breast was, in order to multiply the cries of grief, slaughtered before her eyes.

An impious soldiery scoured the town in fury, athirst for every crime by which pleasure could be given to the tyrant who from sheer love of cruelty had given orders for the massacre of the innocent.

VI. The Hunt is On

At length when the impious Ivar had slain such numbers that he had, I will not say satisfied his Achimenian madness, but from weariness deferred for a while its complete gratification, he summoned a few poor wretches whom he judged to be not worth killing, and by searching cross-examination of them endeavoured to ascertain whereabouts their king was at that time residing.

It seems that a report had reached him that the glorious King Edmund, who was in the prime of life, and in the fullness of vigour, was a keen soldier. On this account Ivar made it his business to cut off all the men whom he could find round about, so that the king, deprived of the support of a compact force for the defence of his kingdom, should be unable to offer effective resistance.

Edmund, it happened, was at that time staying at some distance from the city, in a township which in the native language is called Haegelisdun, from which also the neighbouring forest is called by the same name.

The monster of impiety calculated, as was indeed the truth, that whatever number of the natives his murderous minions could succeed in destroying, so many the less would there be, if it came to a pitched battle, for the king to lead against his foes. Moreover, Ivar did not venture to leave his fleet without a strong guard; for, just as the wolf is accustomed to steal in the evening down to the plains, and to return with haste by night to his lair in the woods, so it was the practice of the Danish and Alanic people, always intent upon a career of theft, never to risk an open and fair fight with their enemies, unless through being entangled in an ambush they had lost all hope of regaining their ships in harbour.

VII. A Saucy Messenger

Accordingly, with excessive caution he summoned one of his array, and despatched him to the king, who was devoid of any such harassing anxiety, with orders to ascertain the amount of his possessions, hoping to take him unawares, as in fact happened, and to daunt him by tortures if he should refuse to comply with the murderous demands of the Dane.

Ivar, accompanied by a great throng, followed in support with leisurely steps. He had given orders to the agent of this wicked mission, thus relieved of all apprehension of danger, to accost the unsuspecting king as follows:

'My august master, and unconquerable sovereign Ivar, a terror by land and sea, having by force of arms brought divers countries into subjection to himself, has landed with a great fleet on the desirable shores of this territory with the intention of firing his winter-quarters here, and in pursuance thereof commands you to share with him your ancient treasures, and your hereditary wealth, and to reign in future under him.

'But if you hold in contempt his power, which is fortified by innumerable battalions, it will be to your own prejudice, as you will be accounted unworthy to live or to reign. And who are you that you should presume to oppose so great a power? The storms and tempests of the deep subserve the purpose of our fleets; and cannot turn from the accomplishment of their settled intentions men who, by grace and favour of the elements, have never suffered injury from the awful thunders of heaven, or from the oft-repeated lightning flash.

'Submit therefore with all your people to this greatest of monarchs whom the elements obey, since he is prepared in his great clemency in all that he undertakes, "To spare the meek, while he o'erwhelms the proud." '

VIII. The King and the Bishop

On hearing this, the most saintly king groaned in profound grief of mind, and hailing one of his bishops, who was his confidential adviser, consulted with him as to the answer which was proper to be returned to the demands preferred. The bishop, alarmed for the safety of the king, used a number of arguments in favour of compliance; but the king, staggered by such advice, and fixing his eyes on the ground, was silent for a little while. Then finally he spoke his mind as follows: 'Bishop, I have reached a point in my life of which I never had any apprehension. See! a barbarous stranger with drawn sword menaces the old occupants of my realm, and the once prosperous natives are reduced to sighs and groans and silence.

'Would that those who now live in dread of perishing by a bloody death might be spared to survive amid the beloved fields of their country, even though I should fall, and that they might in course of time be restored to the brightness of their former prosperity.'

Here the bishop interposed: 'How can you speak of survivors in the land, seeing that the enemy's sword has left scarcely one alive in the whole city? Their axes are blunted with the slaughter of your subjects; you are left without a guard, and they will bind you fast with thongs.

'And therefore, my sovereign, dear to me as my soul, unless you seek safety in flight, or have recourse to the ill-omened alternative of surrender, I fear the tormentors will soon arrive, and you will forfeit your life through the unholy execution of their orders.'

'That,' answered the king, 'is what I desire; that is my dearest wish, not to survive my loyal and dear subjects, who have been bereft of their lives and massacred with their children and their wives as they lay in bed, by a bloodthirsty brigand. And what do you advise? that in life's extremity, bereft of my comrades, I should besmirch my fair fame by taking to flight? I have always avoided the calumnious accusations of the informer; never have I endured the opprobrium of fleeing from the battle- field, realising how glorious it would be for me to die for my country; and now I will of my own free will surrender myself, for the loss of those dear to me has made light itself hateful.

'The Almighty disposer of events is present as my witness that, whether I live or die, nothing shall separate me from the love of Christ, the ring of whose faith I took on me in the sacrament of baptism, when I renounced Satan and all his vanities.

'And by that renunciation it ensued that I gained a triple title to be devoted to the praise and glory of the Eternal Trinity, having been cleansed with a view to the reward of endless life by the anointing of the consecrated chrism.

'Firstly, to wit, I put on the robes proper for the font of healing; in the second place, I received confirmation with the larger episcopal signet; and thirdly, by general acclaim of yourself and the people at large, I acquired the sovereign power of this realm.

'And thus bedewed in threefold manner with the ointment of mystic consecration, I have determined to be the benefactor rather than the ruler of the English

Commonwealth, in scorning to bow my neck to any yoke but that of the service of God.

'It is with a mere pretence of good-will that my cunning foe now spreads the meshes of his machinations, by which he calculates on ensnaring the servant of Christ, above all when he promises that which the divine bounty has already conferred upon me. He allows me life, for which I no longer care; he promises me a kingdom, that I already possess; he would bestow on me riches, of which I have no need. Is it for these things that I am now to begin serving two masters, I who have dedicated myself before my whole court to live and to rule under Christ alone?'

IX. Defiance

Then, turning to the messenger whom the impious Ivar had sent to announce the terms on which his kingdom might be retained, Edmund exclaimed : 'Reeking as you are with the blood of my countrymen, you might justly be doomed to death; but to speak plainly, I would follow the example of Christ my Lord, and refrain from staining my pure hands; and for his name's sake, if the need arise, I am willing and glad to perish by your weapons.

'Therefore return as fast as you can at once to your lord, and take forthwith this message to him:

"Son of the devil, well do you imitate your father, who through his swelling pride fell from heaven, and striving to involve mankind in his falseness, rendered multitudes liable to his punishment.

"You, his chief follower, are powerless to terrify me by threats, nor shall you deceive me with the snares and sophistries that inveigle to destruction, for you will not find me lacking the armour of Christian principles.

"As for the treasures and the wealth, which till now God's favour has bestowed on me, take and squander them as your insatiable greed may prompt, since, even though you should break in pieces this frail and perishable body, like a potter's vessel, my soul, which is truly free, will never for a moment submit to you. For it is more honourable to champion the cause of perpetual freedom, if not with arms, at any rate with life, than to spend tearful complaints in redemanding it when lost, since in the one case death is glorious, but in the other the op- position is but the rebellion of slaves. That is to say, a slave, whatever terms he may have accepted at the hands of his master, is bound to observe them as he accepted them; if he repudiates them, iniquitous though they may be, he is guilty of treason, and is liable to the punishment of a slave.

"But enough; grievous as may be the burden of such a servitude, still more grievous is the rankling sore which misfortune of this kind usually begets, seeing that, as is within the knowledge of those who, as advocates, are practised in the discussion of cases in the law-courts, when a conclusion is deduced from repugnant circumstances, it is certain that, if freedom be aimed at, the tyrant is undoubtedly prejudiced by contempt of himself. Consequently, willingly or unwillingly, let my free spirit wing its way from its prison to heaven, untainted by any appearance of sale or surrender; for be assured, Dane, you shall never see me, a king, survive the loss of freedom to adorn your triumph.

"You ply me with expectations of a continued reign, after the slaughter of all my people, as if I were possessed by so mad a lust of rule, that I could have the heart to reign over houses emptied of their noble inhabitants: their precious garniture. Let your savage ferocity go on as it has begun: after the subjects let the king be snatched from his throne, dragged away, spat upon, struck and buffeted, and finally butchered.

"The King of kings sees all that with compassion, and will, I am confident, translate the victim to reign with him in life eternal. Know, therefore, that for the love of this earthly life Edmund, the Christian king, will not submit to a heathen chief, unless you first become a convert to our religion; he would rather be a standard-bearer in the camp of the Eternal King." '

X. Martyrdom

The saintly man had but just ended his speech, and the soldier taken his departure from the palace to carry back the answer, when, behold! Ivar met him, and bade him waste no words in declaring the final purport of the king's reply.

As the messenger obeyed this behest, the tyrant ordered the crowd of his attendants to form a ring round the place, and to take the king alone prisoner, as showing palpable defiance of the conditions laid down. Then the holy King Edmund was taken in his palace, as a member of Christ, his weapons thrown aside, and was pinioned and tightly bound with chains, and in his innocence was made to stand before the impious general, like Christ before the governor Pilate, and eager to follow in the footsteps of Him who was sacrificed as a victim for us.

And so in chains he was mocked in many ways, and at length, after being savagely beaten, he was brought to a tree in the neighbourhood, tied to it, and for a long while tortured with terrible lashes.

But his constancy was unbroken, while without ceasing he called on Christ with broken voice. This roused the fury of his enemies, who, as if practising at a target, pierced his whole body with arrow-spikes, augmenting the severity of his torment by frequent discharges of their weapons, and

33

inflicting wound upon wound, while one javelin made room for another.

And thus, all haggled over by the sharp points of their darts, and scarce able to draw breath, he actually bristled with them, like a prickly hedgehog or a thistle fretted with spines, resembling in his agony the illustrious martyr Sebastian.

But when it was made apparent to the villainous Ivar that not even by these means could the king be made to yield to the agents of his cruelty, but that he continued to call upon the name of Christ, the Dane commanded the executioner to cut off his head forthwith.

The king was by this time almost lifeless, though the warm life-stream still throbbed in his breast, and he was scarcely able to stand erect. In this plight he was hastily wrenched from the blood-stained stem, his ribs laid bare by numberless gashes, as if he had been put to the torture of the rack, or had been torn by savage claws, and was bidden to stretch forth the head which had ever been adorned by the royal diadem.

Then, as he stood in all his meekness, like a ram chosen out of the whole flock, and desirous of hastening by a happy exchange this life for eternity, absorbed as he was in the mercies of God, he was refreshed by the vision of the light within, for the satisfaction of which he earnestly yearned in his hour of agony. Thus, while the words of prayer were still on his lips, the executioner, sword in hand, deprived the king of life, striking off his head with a single blow.

And so, on the 20th November, as an offering to God of sweetest savour, Edmund, after he had been tried in the fire of suffering, rose with the palm of victory and the crown of righteousness, to enter as king and martyr the assembly of the court of heaven.

XL. Aftermath

Thus in his departure from life, the king, following the footsteps of Christ his master, consummated that sacrifice of the Cross which he had endured continually in the flesh.

Just as Christ, free from all taint of sin, left on the column to which he was bound, not for himself, but for us, the blood which was the mark of his scourging, so Edmund incurred a like penalty bound to the blood-stained tree, for the sake of gaining a glory that fades not away.

Christ, whose life was without stain, suffered in his great benignity the bitter pain of unmerciful nails in his hands and feet in order to cleanse away the foulness of our sins; Edmund, for the love of the holy Name, with his whole body bristling with grievous arrows, and lacerated to the very marrow by the acutest tortures, steadfastly persisted in the avowal of his faith which in the end he crowned by undergoing the doom of death.

The Danes, with their instigator, instruments of the devil, left his body mutilated, as has been described, and transfixed with javelins, while the sacred head, which had been anointed not with the oil of sinners, but with the sacramental chrism of mystery, was carried by them as they retired into a wood, the name of which is Haglesdun, and was thrown as far as possible among the dense thickets of brambles, and so hidden; the Danes contriving this with the greatest cunning, so that the Christians, but few of whom were left alive, should not be able to commit to such decent burial as their limited means of interment would allow, the sanctified body of the martyr conjoined with the head.

XII. A Hunting Party

Of this appalling scene there was present as a spectator, though in hiding, one of our religion, who was rescued, as I believe, by God's providence from the swords of the heathen, and so preserved to bring to light the traces of these events, although he was entirely ignorant what had been done with the head, beyond the fact that he had seen the Danes betaking themselves with it into the depths of the wood.

Accordingly, when peace of some sort had been restored to the churches, the Christians began to emerge from their hiding-places, and to make diligent and busy search with the intention of joining the head of their king and martyr, when found, to the rest of the body, and laying them to rest with due honour according to their means.

And so, on the departure of the heathen, who engaged in the work of devastation elsewhere, the sacred body, still lying above ground, was with no difficulty found in the very field where the king died, when he finished the course of his trial.

Thither, spurred by the recollection of former benefits, and of the gentle nature of their king, the populace, coming together from all directions, began with rueful hearts to lament the loss of so important a part of the body.

Inspiration came by benign suggestion from above; and, after listening to the helpful narrative of the witness who had, as I have said, been a witness of the dreadful scene, they united in great numbers to institute a search in every part of the wood's recesses, in the hope of reaching by hazard the spot where the head of their holy hero was lying.

All who were possessed of true insight were confident that the Danes, as worshippers of strange gods, had out of spite to our faith abstracted the head of the martyr, which they had probably hidden not very far away in the dense thicket, and had left concealed by the coarse undergrowth a prey to birds and beasts.

A council was held, and all unanimously agreed upon a plan; it was decided that each individual should be accoutred with horn or pipe, so that the searchers, in their explorations hither and thither, could by calling or by the noise of their instruments signal one to another, and so avoid going twice over the same ground, or missing some localities altogether.

XIII. Here! Here! Here!

When they carried out this plan, a thing happened marvellous to relate, and unheard of in the course of ages.

The head of the holy king, far removed from the body to which it belonged, broke into utterance without assistance from the vocal chords, or aid from the arteries proceeding from the heart.

A number of the party, like corpse-searchers, were gradually examining the out-of-the-way parts of the wood, and when the moment had arrived at which the sound of the voice could be heard, the head, in response to the calls of the search-party mutually encouraging one another, and as comrade to comrade crying alternately 'Where are you?' indicated the place where it lay by exclaiming in their native tongue, Here! Here! Here! In Latin the same meaning would be rendered by Hic! Hic! Hic!

And the head never ceased to repeat this exclamation, till all were drawn to it. The chords of the dead man's tongue vibrated within the passages of the jaws, thus displaying the miraculous power of Him who was born of the Word, and endowed the braying ass with human speech, so that it rebuked the madness of the prophet.

And to this miracle the Creator of the world added

another by attaching an unwonted guardian to the heavenly treasure. In fact, a monstrous wolf was by God's mercy found in that place, embracing the holy head between its paws, as it lay at full length on the ground, and thus acting as sentinel to the martyr. Nor did it suffer any animal whatever to injure its charge, but, forgetful of its natural ferocity, preserved the head from all harm with the utmost vigilance, lying outstretched on the earth.

This was witnessed with astonishment by the crowd which had assembled, and they recognised in the most blessed king and martyr Edmund a worthy parallel to that enviable man who, unharmed among the gaping jaws of hungry lions, laughed to scorn the threats of those who had plotted his destruction.

XIV. The Saint is Interred

Lifting up, therefore, with concordant devotion the pearl of inestimable price which they had discovered, and shedding floods of tears for joy, they brought back the head to its body, blessing God with hymns and lauds, while the wolf, which was the guardian and bearer of the relic, followed them to the place of entombment, and keeping close behind them, though seemingly grieved for the loss of the pledge it had had in keeping, neither did harm to any one though provoked, nor gave trouble to any one, but again betook itself unharmed to the familiar seclusion of its congenial solitude; and never afterwards was there seen in that neighbourhood any wolf so terrible in appearance.

When the wolf had retired, those who were entrusted with the duty, with the utmost care and with all possible zeal and skill provisionally fitted the head to the sacred body, and committed the two joined together to a becoming sepulchre.

And there they built over the grave a chapel of rude construction, in which the body rested for many years, until the conflagration of war and the mighty storms of persecution were over, and the religious piety of the faithful began to revive, upon relief from the pressure of tribulation. And so, when a seasonable opportunity was found, they displayed in many ways the devotion which they cherished in regard to the blessed king and martyr Edmund.

They were stirred by the occurrence of marvellous works. For the Saint, from beneath the lowly roof of his consecrated abode, made manifest by frequent miraculous signs the magnitude of his merits in the sight of God.

These events aroused great numbers of the inhabitants of that province, high and low alike; and in the royal town which, in the English tongue, is named Bedrices-gueord, but in Latin is called Bedrici-curtis, they erected a church of immense size, with storeys admirably constructed of wood, and to this they translated him with great magnificence, as was due.

XV. Life After Death

But, marvellous to tell, whereas it was supposed that the precious body of the martyr would have mouldered to dust in the long interval of time which had elapsed, it was found to be so sound and whole that it would be out of place to speak of the head having been restored to and united with the body, for there was absolutely no trace apparent of wound or scar.

And so the king and martyr Edmund was with reverence pronounced to be a Saint, and was translated whole and entire, and wearing every semblance of life, to the place above mentioned, where to this day without change of form he awaits the covenanted felicity of a blessed resurrection.

One thing only is to be noticed: round his neck, as an ensign of his martyrdom, there was seen an extremely thin red crease, like a scarlet thread, as was frequently attested by a certain woman of blessed memory called Oswen, who shortly before these recent times of ours passed many years in succession near his consecrated tomb, absorbed in fastings and prayers.

This venerable woman, either from some divine intuition, or from excess of devotion, made it her constant practice to open the sepulchre of the blessed martyr year by year, at the anniversary of the Lord's Supper, and to trim and pare his hair and nails. These relics, one and all, she studiously collected, and stored in a casket; nor did she ever omit, as long as she lived, to cherish them with an affection that was wonderful, having placed them on the altar of the church to which I have referred.

And there they are still preserved with due veneration.

XVI. Eight Thieves

There is, moreover, the evidence of Theodred of blessed memory, the pious bishop of the province, whose good deserts challenged for him the designation of 'the good'.

He verified, as is set out below, the fact which I have stated of the incorruption of the sainted king. Divers persons in their piety had contributed, as I had begun to relate, a number of offerings and ornaments in gold and silver of great value, to the place above mentioned as having been selected for the entombment of the martyr, when some men of depraved minds, and utterly forgetful of what was right, attempted under cover and in the silence of night to break into the temple of the king for the purpose of robbery.

There were eight of these marauders who, totally wanting in reverence for the Saint, had determined to gratify their crazy cupidity by the theft of everything which they might find of use to themselves within the precincts of the monastery. They furnished themselves accordingly with whatever implements and tools they had that would be serviceable for the execution of this work, and one night attempted to carry out their premeditated crime. Posted in the fore-court of the church, each member of the gang applied himself in his several capacity to his share of the concerted outrage.

Thus one laid a ladder to the door-posts, in order to climb through the window; another was engaged with a file, or a smith's hammer, on the bars and bolts; others with shovels and mattocks endeavoured to undermine the walls. The work being thus distributed, whilst they vied one with another in the most strenuous exertions, the holy martyr bound them fast in the midst of their efforts, so that they could neither stir from the spot nor abandon the task upon which they had entered; one on his ladder hung aloft in mid-air, another was displayed to view with his back bent in digging, who had stolen unobserved to the guilty deed.

Meanwhile, one of the staff of attendants who was sleeping within the temple, though aroused from his slumbers, was kept a prisoner in his bed, restrained in his endeavour to rise by the martyr's power, so that no sound or noisy echo should reach the ears of the custodian within, and so impede the manifestation of the Saint's miraculous power.

But I understate the facts when I say that the man could not rise, seeing that he could not so much as utter a word. At length morning came, and then the thieves, still persevering with the work which they had begun, were arrested by a number of people, and, after being firmly secured by chains, were finally committed to the above-mentioned holy bishop Theodred for trial.

The bishop, through inadvertence, pronounced upon them a sentence of which he afterwards regretted the infliction for the whole of his life-time. In fact, he ordered the whole gang to be hanged together, because, for the purpose of theft, they had dared to invade the precincts of St. Edmund the Martyr.

But he failed to keep in mind the monition of God through his prophet, 'Cease not to deliver those who are appointed to die,' and the action of Elisha the Prophet, who fed the robbers of Samaria with bread and water, and sent them to their own homes, saying to the king who was minded to slay them on the spot, that he had not taken them by means of his sword and his bow; and again, the injunction of the Apostle, in which he says, 'If then ye have judgements of things pertaining to this life, set them to judge who are least esteemed in the Church,' meaning thereby laymen.

This is the origin of the canonical precept which forbids a bishop or any one in holy orders to discharge the function of an informer, as it is highly unbecoming that the ministers of the heavenly life should yield assent to the death of any man whatever.

Consequently the bishop aforesaid, when he reflected on what he had done, was struck with profound remorse, and awarded penance against himself, remaining for a long while engrossed in deep contrition.

At the end of his penance he issued a proclamation to the inhabitants of his diocese, and by the proclamation he convened them, and in convening, he begged and entreated them, by means of a three days' fast, to remove and avert from him the divine indignation and wrath, to the end that the Lord, being appeased by the sacrifice of a troubled spirit, should accord him grace, by which he might venture to touch and wash the body of the blessed martyr, who, though he blossomed with so many virtues when in the world, was nevertheless enshrined in a poor sepulchre, inadequate to his deserts.

And so it was done; and the bishop found the body of the most holy king, which before had been lacerated and mutilated, as I have already related, whole and incorrupt; he handled it, he washed it, he clothed it afresh with new robes of the best, and replaced it in a wooden coffin, blessing God, who is wonderful in His saints and glorious in all His works.

47

XVII. Leofric

I shall not, I hope, tire my readers if I mention the fate of a
man of great position named Leofstan, who, unable to curb
the impetuosity of youth, was carried to such a pitch of
wanton wickedness that he demanded, in the exercise of his
supreme authority, the exhibition to himself of the martyr's
body.

Although he was dissuaded by many persons, and
chiefly by his own retainers, his command prevailed, as he
was regarded with general dread on account of the pre-
eminence of his rank. The coffin was opened; he stood by,
he looked in, and at that very moment the Lord smote him
with madness and gave him over to a reprobate mind.

Thus he was taught by his punishment that his
presumption had carried him beyond lawful bounds. This
came to the ears of his father, a man of deep piety, whose
name was Ælfgar. He was appalled by the infamous crime of
his son; and rendered thanks to the martyr, and turned his
son out of doors. The latter was reduced at length to the
depths of poverty, and by God's judgement was devoured by
worms, and so brought his life to an end.

XVIII. Body and Soul

In such wise the holy king and martyr, Edmund, demonstrated to the world that he was not inferior in merit to Lawrence, the blessed deacon and martyr.

As has been related by the blessed Pope Gregory, certain persons, worthy or unworthy, inspected his body with the intention of exhuming it, and out of their number it befell that no less than eight perished on the spot by sudden death.

Oh! what deep reverence was due to that place, which contains in the guise of one asleep so august a witness to Christ, and in which such wondrous works are said to have occurred, and do occur, as in these times we have heard of in no other part of England! For brevity's sake I pass over these, not being desirous of incurring by undue prolixity the resentment of any fastidious person, and in the belief that what has been related will satisfy the ardent wishes of those who deem nothing preferable to the patronage of this martyr, except God himself.

It is fully proved in his case (as in that of all the other saints who already reign with Christ) that though his spirit be in the enjoyment of heavenly glory, yet it has power to revisit the body and is not by day or night far separated from the place where that body lies, in union with which it has earned the joys of a blessed immortality, of which even now it has the fruition.

Doubtless, in its eternal home, where it is united to Him, who is integrally present every- where, the spirit has from Him power proportioned to its capacity of will, besides the boon of boons which it covets with unwearying desire, that by the resurrection it should be enveloped with the garment of the flesh transformed; since then will the beatitude of the saints be perfected, when that consummation shall have been attained through the bounty of Christ.

XIX. Purity

And how great was the holiness in this life of the holy martyr may be conjectured from the fact that his body even in death displays something of the glory of the resurrection with- out trace of decay; for it must be borne in mind that they who are endued with this kind of distinction are extolled by the Catholic Fathers in the rolls of their religion as having attained the peculiar privilege of virginity, for they teach that such as have preserved their chastity till death, and have endured the stress of persecution even to the goal of martyrdom, by a just recompense are endued even here on earth, when death is past, with incorruption of the flesh.

What, indeed, can be thought a higher privilege in the dispensation of love and Christian faith than this, that mortal man should acquire by grace the attribute which angels have by nature? So it is that the divine oracle promises as by a peculiar concession that the Virgins shall follow the Lamb whithersoever He goeth.

Let us then consider what manner of man he was, who, stationed on the royal throne in the midst of worldly wealth and luxury, strove to conquer self, by treading under foot all carnal desires, as is shown by the incorruptibility of his flesh.

And let those who render to him the ministry of human reverence strive to the utmost to please him by that purity of life, which his uncorrupted body proves to have been his continual happiness; and, if they cannot do so with the flower of virgin modesty, let them at least steadfastly mortify their desire for pleasure, of which they have had past experience.

For should the Presence of that sacred spirit, which no eye can detect, and which is not confined by limits of space, be offended by the foul life of any of his ministers, it is to be feared that, according to the dreadful threat of the prophet, 'He hath done iniquity in the land of the saints, and therefore shall not see the glory of the Lord.'

Feeling the terror of such a doom, let us implore the protection of Saint Edmund, king and martyr, that he may deliver us, and all those who worthily minister to him, from those sins for which we deserve to be punished, through Him who lives and reigns, world without end, Amen.

Here ends the Passion of Saint Edmund, King and Martyr.

Select Bibliography

Carlyle, Thomas: *Past and Present (Collected Works Volume XIII)*, Chapman & Hall, 1843

Hegge, John and Webb, Simon: *The Legend of St Cuthbert*, Langley Press, 2013

Hervey, Francis (ed.): *Corolla Sancti Eadmundi*, John Murray, 1907

Houghton, Bryan: *Saint Edmund King and Martyr*, Terence Dalton, 1970

Lydgate, John: *Poems*, Oxford, 1966

Lydgate, John and Webb, Simon: *The Legend of St Alban*, Langley Press, 2016

Renoir, Alain: *The Poetry of John Lydgate*, Routledge & Kegan Paul, 1967

Webb, Simon: *In Search of the Northern Saints*, Langley Press, 2018

Weston, Jessie: *From Ritual to Romance*, Doubleday, 1957

Wolffe, Bertram, *Henry VI*, Yale, 1981

Made in the USA
Middletown, DE
08 October 2020

21447589R00031